GREATEST TOOL FOR ATTRACTING WEBSITE TRAFFIC	**1**
CREATE GREAT ONLINE PRESENCE FOR MAXIMUM VISITORS	3
HOW TO DEVELOP A PROMOTIONAL NETWORK	5
FABULOUSLY INCREASING YOUR SUBSCRIBERS Via E-mail and Fax	7
YOUR QR SMART CODE	9
HIGH-PRICED DOMAINS	11
BILLION DOLLAR PHRASE	13
NEW DOMAIN EXTENSIONS	15
HOW TO BUY DOMAIN NAMES	17
HOW TO BUY NEW gTLDS	19
HOW TO EXCEL AT SEO	21
HOW THE INTERNET WAS TAKEN	24
KEY TO SUCCESS IN BUYING DOMAINS	26
FREE MARKET DOMAIN ILLUSIONS	30
SEO CLASSIFIED FILES	32
HOW TO BE NUMBER #1 ON GOOGLE	34
TIPS TO INCREASE WEBSITE SPEED	36
DOMAIN INTERNET CHANGES	38
HOW TO BE A DOMAIN PROFESSIONAL	40
DOMAIN NAME MADNESS	42
INTERNET EXPANSION FUNDING	44
NEW gTLDs Trademark Concerns	46
DOMAIN EXCHANGE	48
SOCIAL MEDIA SYNDROME	50
WEBINERD	52
WORLD OF BLOGS	**54**
WEBSITE SUCCESS TIPS	56
AD WORDS OPTIONS	57

GREATEST TOOL FOR ATTRACTING WEBSITE TRAFFIC

Greatest tool for attracting website traffic is diversity of content and a unique image that shows you are upbeat. Diversity of content can include articles on a variety of topics, lists of projects completed and any media details about your achievements. Having a link to your website displayed on another website is a great way to receive traffic to your website. But your website link should be correctly positioned on the hosting website. If possible, include your website at the bottom of an article that shows you to be a capable expert on a set topic.

When writing the article you should consider that while it needs to be informative it should also be interesting and written using plain language. Also, try to use upbeat language and write the content in a way that will be perceived positively by your reader. Use puns and jokes sparingly. But humor is definitely a plus for your article to be happily received by your readership. In your article, make references to other experts and their work. You might not want to direct your readers to other experts that might upstage you. But this should not concern you. Listing other experts on the set topic will demonstrate your full knowledge of the topic and the relevant commentators on it. Possibly by listing these experts will result in them doing the same for you in their articles and on their website.

Make sure that your website has a reciprocal link to the website listing your article. Create as many reciprocal links as possible. You should also list social media achievements; such as being a highly ranked user of a social media platform and being a contributor to it. Having many friends / connections is a major plus in today's online social media age. Therefore, your presented reputation will increase according to the increase in friends or connections you have. Reputation management is a key component of digital marketing and recognition of your website. Visitors go towards popular businesses. Ensure the popularity of your website by building a strong presence for your brand. Online is like the real world. Your brand speaks for your company. If it is well liked, then your business will be popular and your website often visited by many new prospective clients. Relevance of your business connections is a key to them being positively endorsed and branded. This is the greatest tool for attracting website traffic.

CREATE GREAT ONLINE PRESENCE FOR MAXIMUM VISITORS

After you have built your website or blog - customizing it with social media capability and so forth - you need to make it visitor worthy. You might believe that your website or blog is interesting and that is reason enough for visitors to initially land on your page. But you need to be distinguishable from every other similar and unrelated website or blog. You need to be the diamond of websites / blogs.

To reach this pinnacle, or jewel-like status on the internet, you need to have a colorful and welcoming website. Not too much text, at least on the main page. That is, unless of course your website is meant for the purpose of broadcasting events, or promotions. If you have too much text, then your readers will be overwhelmed with a plethora of information. Conversely if you do not have enough writing on your website, then your followers will have no reason to return to your website or blog. Perhaps that clear distinction between a website and a blog is an important place to start the discussion on how to develop and maintain your online presence. While a blog contains a biography of the blogger and regular posts on a specific topic(s), a website has a distinctive marketing structure. A website might also contain blog posts. But posts are not the main focus of the website.

Blogs and websites alike have subscribers who are interested in receiving regular written posts from the web portal. To maintain or increase the readership of your posts, you will need to write interesting articles on a variety of topics. Most importantly, your writing should be consistent. You can compose new posts daily, or weekly. But be consistent. Readers will want to establish a routine of reading your posts. To ensure readers want to read what you have written, keep your sentences short and your thoughts concise. Consider popular trends and emerging topics when composing your topics. It is best to write about a theme that is in the media, online or otherwise. Or for a blog, you might choose to often write an evolving series of poems or short stories. Whatever you write should be clear and to the point. Usually website / blog readers peruse a post and might just scan the page for keywords that they find to be appealing.

HOW TO DEVELOP A PROMOTIONAL NETWORK

Consider the market of the business professionals with whom you want to network. If you really want to know how to develop a promotional network then survey business professionals with whom you want to build a promotional network. Ask them: what topics are of interest to them? Write about their services and products. Compose articles that you know they would enjoy reading and which would appeal to their customers.

Writing articles of value, for your professional network, will increase the likelihood of them promoting and circulating your literary masterpieces. Consider topics that promote their products and services in new ways. Incorporating new slogans or prose into the editorial, along with humor, will surely enrich the worth of the document.

Businesses are always appreciative of complementary text, which illuminates their company. Before composing your written material, speak directly with the principal of the business to determine what topics would make for an interesting critique. Also, inquire as to whether or not humor or puns would be acceptable for inclusion in the commentary. Read current publications about the business, written by them or by journalists. Review the style of those compositions and keep them in mind, when creating your article.

Write two versions of your document. One edition should be created using industry relevant marketing terms and one version, in vernacular, or plain language. This way the company will have the option of varied texts. Perhaps they will use one copy in a trade related magazine and the other on their website or in their newsletter.

Contemporary businesses want to read articles that have been written with industry specific jargon. Whereas, customers want to read text that is both intriguing and exciting. Writing, while considering the audience of readership, will aid you in focusing on key points of curiosity. That being said, if you are going to write numerous articles for the same company, then you should limit your text to one focal point. Therefore, you will be able to write many articles without your documents seeming redundant.

A great way to develop a promotional network is by hosting events; either online events known as virtual events, or onsite events. During focused events that have a clear theme and set program for mingling and networking, business professionals can meet and interact. A large glass bowl at the entrance to the event for business professionals to leave their company business card is an excellent strategy. Perhaps a business card draw with a prize is the best idea to encourage event attendees to deposit their business card in the large bowl for the raffle.

FABULOUSLY INCREASING YOUR SUBSCRIBERS Via E-mail and Fax

- *Compose regular articles on com, which you should share on Facebook.com, Google+, StumbleUpon.com, Tumblr.com and Twitter.com; among other social media outlets. You could post a notice within each article encouraging comments from readers, which will ensure an increasing amount of regular followers. You could even suggest subscribers should compose relevant posts about Jewish topics on LinkedIn.com and ask them to mention your organization and your newsletter and / or provide a link to it, within their posts. Here is a relevant and inspiring article I composed wherein I could promote your organization and newsletter, entitled the: Fabulous Ten Thousand – Are You One? This article was read by 105 people so far. On LinkedIn.com I currently have 1070 subscribers to my posts. I grew this fan base over the last few months.*

- *Create a Facebook.com group specifically for increasing subscribers. Here subscribers can share anecdotes about Jewish life, including; Shabbat dinners, recipes, travel tips and et cetera. Subscribers to this group can like the group and recommend / suggest the group to friends. Once a member likes your group their status of liking will appear in their public feed on their wall. The trend of liking will only continue to grow and increase exponentially.*

- *Mitzvah Points for subscribers who suggest 50 or more friends who become subscribers. After an accumulation of a certain number of mitzvah points, high-ranking subscribers can request a letter from you noting the total points to date, which can be redeemed at local participating kosher restaurants for a complimentary meal. Alternatively, mitzvah points could be redeemed for online* *purchases of Jewish lifestyle products, such as; Candles, Menorahs, Tallisim, Tefillin, Tzitzit and so forth. Obviously the points would not have an actual monetary value. 50 points would not equal $50. But the points could be used towards a discount of a certain percentage off of the purchase price, with participating Jewish businesses.*

- *To increase subscribers you could also ask Mitzvah Points partners to like your organization on social media and to provide you with the e-mail addresses of their customers who have provided an authorization for the same. You could post a link to your newsletter on the participating businesses' website or have a promotional contact form for potential subscribers to complete, in order to receive your newsletter.*

- *You could also have a picture contest for Jewish themes, with a small entry fee for contestants; along with a great prize for the winner. You could ask major Jewish businesses / organizations to donate prize(s) or in-kind products / services. Each competitor would submit their complete contact information when entering the contest and simultaneously agree to receive emails or faxes from you.*

- *You could distribute tzedakah boxes internationally that could be donated to your organization, via local banks; to be deposited into a bank account, specifically set up for this purpose. The tzedakah boxes could be adorned with a sticky notepad that has an embossed watermark with your website link and the words: "Thank you for your support". Donors could note down a promissory donation amount on the sticky note for future donation commitments. Also a tick-able (checkmark notation) of daily, weekly or monthly donation amounts could be affixed around the tzedakah box for donors to note their regular donation amounts. Alternatively a few options of donation charts could accompany the tzedakah box, which could be affixed by adhesive (glue) to the tzedakah box.*

YOUR QR SMART CODE

Nowadays potential and current customers want to know everything about your business instantly; with one click on a mobile device, if possible. No waiting period is acceptable. Bar codes and Quick Response (QR) Codes[1] are all the hype; by offering complete details about your company at the speed of light. Here, light speed is meant to explain the time taken for a laser or light beam to immediately scan the QR or Barcode and read the data contained in it.

Is it a good idea to put all information about a business in a code? If you want potential customers to be able to show up at your office or production location, then it is perhaps alright to include the geographical or 'brick and mortar' address in the QR code. If you want potential customers to find your company on the World Wide Web, then you would want to include your website address in the Code. You could also include text that contains a brief synopsis of your business operations and a tagline or promotional text.

Every person, just like every business, also has a QR Code or Barcode. Everyone has an identifier by which they are known at first glance. There are a few set characteristics by which one is categorized, defined and also evaluated. One's economic standing, ancestry, ethnicity, appearance and personality all shape the perception others have of oneself. At one glance one is 'sized up' and processed in people's minds.

Other factors can also determine the impression one leaves on others, such as; how one greet others, the inflection or projection of one's voice, one's posture and the stride of one's step. One can walk in so many varied ways that there are more than 60 styles of walking.[1] Everything about oneself provides an explanation of who one seems to be, either in actuality, or least in the mind's eye perception that others have about oneself.

Does one's self-perception affect or influence how others see oneself? Does charisma play a role in one's self-estimation and in the valuation of one by others? Your calling card to the world is your QR Code. How you look and how you speak – even more than what you say – may speak volumes about who you are in the view of others. Be sure that you know your QR Code and be certain that you are displaying the characteristics you want to be read, at first glance / scan.

[1] http://www.dailywritingtips.com/60-synonyms-for-walk

HIGH-PRICED DOMAINS

Before purchasing a domain name it is best to perform a trademark search, on a tag line, domain name, and / business name that you plan to use; since you do not want to infringe on the intellectual property of a company. It might seem difficult to believe, but some businesses actually own the right to certain keywords, terms, phrases, slogans and concepts. There are upwards of 250 domain extensions.[1] Also, there is a vast list - ranging upwards, to 70 or more - of abbreviations for the domain name industry.[2]

Some currently listed high-priced domains, at auction, fetch upwards of $185K to more than $35 million dollars.

Some of the Highest-Priced Domains:

- VacationRentals.com $35 million in 2007
- Insure.com $16 million in 2009
- Fund.com 2008 £9.99 million
- Business.com for $7.5 million in 1999
- Diamond.com 2006 $7.5 million
- Beer.com 2004 $7 million
- Israel.com 2008 $5.88 million
- GiftCard.com by CardLab for $4 million in 2012
- Yp.com by YellowPages.com for $3.8 million in 2008
- AltaVista.com for $3.3 million in 1998
- Candy.com for $3.0 million in 2009
- Loans.com by Bank of America for $3.0 million in 2000. [3]

Before buying a domain one can have its value appraised. Be cautious as to which domain appraisal website you use, as some are more accurate than others. While some evaluators utilize key word frequency and balance these against the number of searches on the phrase, others assessors are totally arbitrary and the valuation is unreliable.

Recently, Registrars on the Internet began releasing the first batch of nearly two thousand new domain extensions; including everything from dot beer to dot health. Any combination of phrases and keywords is possible within the domain name and as combined with the extension.

The release of these domain extensions is due in part to hoarding of domain names and trademark infringement. Many domain entrepreneurs bought up many domain names that represent and express the brand of an existing business, with the intention to sell the same domain name to the business whose name is part of the domain name.

Many small, medium and large business owners and corporations complained about this seeming injustice, while being unwilling to pay the sought after price to acquire a domain name that contains their own business brand. In the past businesses could complain to the United States Congress, which used to monitor and regulate the Internet. Now the Internet is managed by a consortium, known as the Madrid Conference, which is supposed to be an organization operating as an independent entity and totally separate from any government jurisdiction, but which is seemingly accountable to the United Nations.

New domain extensions and new domains registered at the same time are now monitored and processed through a clearinghouse that accepts trademark registrations and holds or blocks potential domain registrations, which may infringe on the said trademark.

---

[1] http://www.allacronyms.com/tag/domain_name
[2] http://www.abbreviations.com/acronyms/DOMAINNAMES
[3] http://en.wikipedia.org/wiki/List_of_most_expensive_domain_names

BILLION DOLLAR PHRASE

Is there such a thing as a billion dollar phrase? Can a domain name be worth a million dollars or a billion dollars? Domain names have sold for millions of dollars in the past and will likely do so well into the future. Knowing which domain name is a valuable catch phrase is like trying to predict the winning numbers in the lottery.

Is foresight of the optimal combinations of letters, symbols, numbers and / or words possible? Your ability to be creative in combination with your level of intelligence will determine your domain name savviness. You need to be able to figure out which popular or emerging trends will have a value for a business or organization.

Let us suppose that you are capable of conceiving of the most popular phrase and you are able to buy a domain name at the most relevant extension to accompany it. Does this ensure that you will be able to rank the domain name highly on Search Engines? Will you be able to sell advertising space on it or be able to sell the domain name and / or website to a business or organization?

Even if the domain name is relevant to a specific industry or business area there is no guarantee that you can convince others of the applicable value. Moreover, can you be certain that the domain name is not trademarked by a company in your country of residence and / or internationally? That is right. There are international trademark registrations. But how can you search these words or phrases globally?

The World Intellectual Property Organization is a great place to start your worldwide search for protected trademarks. These links are useful:

- http://www.wipo.int/madrid/en/how_to/search/
- http://www.wipo.int/reference/en/index.html#databases
- http://www.wipo.int/reference/en/branddb/
- http://www.wipo.int/branddb/en/

If the prospective domain name and extension are available for registration without infringement implications, then you still need to be sure that you will be able to properly pre-register or priority pre-register your new generic top-level domain name. There are also various phases that are based on the proximity or nearness of the date of public release of the domain name, which can be subscribed to for the right price(s). Therefore, the greater your budget and the more daring you hope to be the more likely your chances of securing your desired domain name. To find out release dates for new generic top-level domains this website seems to be a great reference:

https://www.webnames.ca/domain-registration/new-domain-name-launch-schedule.aspx

NEW DOMAIN EXTENSIONS

Are you as confused and excited about the new TLDs (Top-Level Domains) as I am?

With so many new domain extensions to potentially be released - up to 700 - how can you not be enthralled at this massive change to the online world?

But when are these domain extensions going to be available to the public? Is there a schedule or timeline? What will be the cost per domain and extension? Who will set the prices? Earlier today I spoke with a representative who told me that the domain extensions will be divided and assigned to various registrars. I was not able to obtain anymore information other than finding out that there are updates about available about the domain expansion, which can be viewed on the following links:

- http://www.icann.org/en/news/press/materials
- http://www.icann.org/en/news/press/releases/release-23oct13-en

If you scroll to the bottom of either of the pages to be found on the links noted above, then you can sign-up to stay connected to receive updates, such as news alerts, newsletters and much more.

To find out the status of any of the new TLDs (Top Levels Domains or Extensions) search the extension on this link:
https://gtldresult.icann.org/application-result/applicationstatus

It is interesting to note that initially 1930 applications were submitted for approval of new Top Level Domains.

According to Marcaria.com: "With the new gTLD program approximately 1,500 new extensions will be launched between the end of 2013 and the end of 2015."

According to Godaddy.com: "The competition for some of the new domains will be fierce. So to increase your chances of getting the domain name you want, we suggest you pre-register. For all pre-registration phases, GoDaddy will automatically submit your application to the registry the instant the phase opens. Which means you'll be at the front of the line to claim your new name." Godaddy proclaims that "With the introduction of new **gTLDs**, you have a fresh chance to get the domain name you really want. Because many of the new domain extensions are specific to particular industries, interests, or locations your web address can now tell people exactly what you do (or where you do it). This makes the new domains easy to remember and easier to find online."

Here you can find the list of New Domains or New gTLDs organized by categories, alphabetically, and/or by status. New domain names are available for almost every industry. Having a domain name at top level generic domain name extension is an optimal way to rank your website.

HOW TO BUY DOMAIN NAMES

Domaining is an intense process of contemplating, buying & selling great domain names. In this seemingly simple, but actually highly complex realm, acquiring and marketing your domain is a sophisticated process. Want to know how to be a domain professional?

Firstly, you need to decide if you are going to create a short domain of one to two letters and such. Then you must evaluate if you should create a more specific longer phrase domain name that actually means something and is perhaps the name of a company or process. Next you have to buy it at the right price, which is not always the lowest cost. Since after you purchase the domain it will be locked with a registrar for sixty days and during that time period you will need to rely on the service and customer support of the registrar. Therefore, you will want to buy from a dependable seller who will assist you once you have bought the domain. Particulars such as functionality of an e-mail address and domain forwarding are considerations that you will want to take into account before you pay for your online address.

Secondly, how marketable is your newly acquired domain name? Can you resell it for more than you paid to buy it? If so, by what markup? Who is your intended demographic for sale? What sale price is reasonable? When listing your domain for sale it is a good idea to have a comprehensive concept to match the domain. Otherwise, unless the domain is ultimately catchy as a key phrase, no one will want to buy it for more than you spent to purchase it. Once aware of the domain name, a prospective buyer might opt to buy the same domain name with a varied extension, such as dot.org, dot.biz or others. Therefore, you should buy all of the possible extensions for your domain at the initial time of purchase or definitely before marketing your domain.

Thirdly, it is important to know if your domain name has value. There are websites that evaluate the worth of a domain. But it is more important to know the inherent value of the domain name to your intended buyers. Now that close to seven hundred new extensions will be released worldwide, having a great domain has never been easier. Many domain registrars are pre-registering customers for their dream domain name. At last count, one such registry had nearly two million pre-registrations. You should consider the best extension for your domain by utilizing part of your domain name as the extension itself.

Lastly, in this rigmarole of domaining, having the right budget is the key to being successful. After you have pre-registered for countless names, you will have to pay for them once they become available. Also, after you have purchased many domains, you need to be sure you will have enough money to buy more domains and to meet your general expenses. Having a reserve account for expenditures, in addition to investors and partners is a good idea. Even though you will need to share the potential profits, you will have more cushions on which to rely. It is important to note that the governing organization for domains has recently created a trademark clearinghouse. Therefore, it is wise to research the current usage of a phrase before buying it to avoid infringing on the intellectual property of someone else.

HOW TO BUY NEW gTLDS

United States Cedes Regulation of Internet to a Foreign Entity. See this link for details: NYTimes.com. Exactly how to buy a new gTLD (generic Top Level Domain) is something of a mystery. So it seems, from a basic inquiry into new extension registrations that one can pre-register for approximately fifty dollars and priority pre-register for nearly four hundred dollars. Neither process ensures that one will actually be able to acquire a domain name at a new extension. Instead, after paying the so-called pre-registration or priority pre-registration fee, one enters into a cue to potentially compete for a new domain at a new extension. If one decides to bow out and not bid for their new extension, then one forfeits an application fee of approximately one hundred and sixty dollars. The actual contents or required details for the application only being reviewable once one has paid the noted fees.

     You may even pre-register a domain name at one of the nearly two thousand new generic top level domain name extensions. If there are multiple pre-registrants, then your proposed domain name will go to auction, which usually lasts seven days or so. You may be bidding against other competitors at the same Internet Domain Registrar. A domain name registrar sells domain names on behalf of registries who actually create the domain name extension. If priority pre-registration was permitted for your chosen domain extension, then the priority pre-registration trumps all general pre-registrations. If there are multiple priority pre-registrations from different registrants at various registrars, then the auction will take place among these competitors.

     You would be smart or wise to consult with a domain broker and Intellectual Property Lawyer who specializes in Internet matters before buying a domain name. This will hopefully ensure that you do not have any issues later on. Apparently there is no actual regulation of the new gTLDs by anyone other than the registry of the gTLD. The registry can manage the potential auction for a domain name at a new extension once it ensues and potentially the highest bid would become the property of the registry. What if multiple registrars are accepting pre-registrations for the same domain at the same gTLD? How will the auction be managed? Information on this process can be found one these links:

gtldresult.icann.org/application-result/applicationstatus or icann.org/en/news & icann.org/en/news/press/materials. View comments about the internet and create one at: icann.org/en/news/public-comment

HOW TO EXCEL AT SEO

To successfully promote your website online and maximize search engine optimization, you need to utilize a variety of tools. Knowing how to excel at SEO (search engine optimization) is essential to online success.

Using SEO in combination with Social Media promotion will greatly enhance the presence of your website on the World Wide Web. To achieve long-term ranking results you will need to regularly update and promote your website.

Even though there are some people who offer the opinion that Meta-Tags are obsolete, they are actually quite useful for search engines to rank and index websites. Having a meta-tag tool on your website is definitely a great idea. Also, you will want to register your website with Google and benefit from Google Analytics to track your website. You also want to verify your website with Google Webmaster tools and link your verified website with your tracking. Inserting the tracking code can be a challenge if your website is a WordPress website. There are many plug-ins available to help make this process easier.

You will also want to verify your website with Bing and import a site map here, as well. Registering your website with Alexa is also very important to ensure that visitors can view your website's ranking and status. Speaking of making things easy, you will want to write about your website, within its pages and circulate articles about your business and services to other websites, as well; all the while noting your website and provide a link to it within the article.

Creating shared links with your website, another similar or related business are also super valuable suggestions to increasing your websites ranking. Search engines rank websites according to connectivity of websites with other websites, which is known as creating referral links, backlinks and crosslinks. Also by submitting your website to Search Engines - through a wide range of website submission services - is the optimal way to increase the ranking of your website and maximise online exposure.

I note many options for you to create an online presence. I list a variety of website tools to utilize.

Resources for Website Ranking:

- http://www.freemetataggenerator.com/

Google Analytics / Tracking Code Google Webmaster Tools / Verified

- http://www.google.com/analytics/
- http://www.bing.com/toolbox/webmaster
- http://www.seo-lab.com/directory-articles/best-free-directories.php
- http://www.wowdirectory.com/
- http://www.alexa.com/
- http://www.bing.com/toolbox
- linkmarket.com,
- www.hotvsnot.com
- http://jayde.com/
- http://www.submitterbot.com/
- http://www.entireweb.com/free_submission/
- http://www.submitexpress.com/free-submission.html
- http://www.dmoz.org/help/submit.html
- http://www.websiteurlsubmission.com
- http://submitstart.com,

- http://www.searchenginecolossus.com/
- http://www.freewebsubmission.com/
- http://www.webs.com/blog/2011/12/06/20-free-places-to-promote-your-website-online/

HOW THE INTERNET WAS TAKEN

It might seem strange to suggest that something intangible as the internet could be taken. But that is exactly what is happening and has happened so far. Initially new domain extensions (gTLDs – generic Top-Level Domains) were so highly priced that an average person could not afford to purchase one. Eventually prices were reduced to permit more people to purchase domain at the gTLD. By the time the extension was reasonably affordable, being sold for ten dollars to fifteen dollars, on average, with some registrar's charging more and other less for the first initial domain and exorbitant amounts for any additional domains. To restart the process, to be fair registries were permitted to create seven hundred new gTLDs. This new allocation of gTLDs should allow for a fair distribution of new gTLDs so everyone can buy the domain name they want. I think not.

Now, with the largest internet revolution and expansion in history occurring, it is unclear how the prices are set for the new gTLDs. Moreover, who is overseeing or managing the process of assignment of gTLDs to registrars and who sets the prices or determines the timing of the *sunrise date* / phase (dates when participants are required to register and validate their trademarks) are matters of obscurity for the consumer. Who determines the advance purchase date of payment for arranging pre-registration with an assigned registrar? Also, it is important to know the decision is made, to determine which registrar's will be assigned which gTLD's? Will trademarked names be excluded from purchase? Will premium domain names at new gTLDs be scooped by registrars or auctioned directly by the registries at unfathomable prices?

Even after pre-registering a domain at a new gTLD one will need to wait until the actual date of registration to find out if their chosen domain name was successfully registered. Registration dates can range from being four to six months away from the pre-registration dates. If domain (buying and selling domains) is your business, it is of much interest to you how the price is set for gTLD and the governance of the administration process for new extensions. With some registrars supposedly being uniquely assigned set gTLDs, while others claiming that they have the right to pre-register extensions that they have not yet been assigned, the process of new gTLD acquisition is quite complicated. How does a consumer know who to trust with their money? One registrar is charging approximately fifty dollars for pre-registration of a new gTLD and nearly four hundred dollars for pre—pre-registration. The difference between the two options supposedly being that the pre-pre-registration option will have your application for a new domain at a newly released extension being submitted to the managing registry a few days before registration opens. While a pre-registered domain application will only be submitted on the days that the gTLD is available to be registered.

KEY TO SUCCESS IN BUYING DOMAINS

To be able to afford a new gTLD is a near impossibility for the average person. The major issue for those who have the financial resources to buy a new gTLD is being able to know the actual sunrise date set by the registry and the actual date that an assigned registrar will be selling the gTLD. Knowing the potential sunrise date of a new extension is not a straightforward process. Registrars seem either unsure of when the registry will assign the gTLD to them and which gTLDs will be assigned to which registrars.

This madness needs to become sane for the sake of the domain game. Perhaps registrars could set up an optioned system; whereby they would accept payments, at any time before the sunrise dates, for new gTLDs. Then on the sunrise date, when the domain name can actually be pre-registered, convert the held payment to a received payment for pre-registration. This way a customer can rest assured in the hope that they will not need to watch the forum on a registrars' website to find out when a new gTLD will be available for pre-registration. Since by the time the gTLD is announced for sale, it will be too late to secure the domain name one wants to purchase; as one will be competing second by second with other customers at the same registrar. This process is not in isolation, as one will also be in stark competition with customers at one of six other potential registrars to whom the same gTLD might have been assigned. Unbeknownst to the average consumer some domain names will not be assigned to registrars. These premium domains will be managed directly by the registry who will sell them at their own private auctions.

When will the madness end? Is there no governance of this new process for new gTLDs? For the large corporations, who will be first in line to secure nearly six hundred of the seven hundred new gTLDs, there is a process that is being securely managed to ensure that those with the deepest pockets get the extension they want. As well, if you can afford nearly four hundred dollars for a pre-registration of a domain name at a new extension that you may or may not actually be able to buy, then you can also play the domain game. If your application is unsuccessful you will not receive a refund for your so-called application fee, being one hundred and sixty dollars or so.

Even if your application is successful, you might need to enter into a bidding competition with other seemingly successful potential buyers for a new domain name at new gTLD. If you choose not to bid or cannot maintain your bids and thereby withdraw from the process you will forfeit your application fee. If you bid and the bid amount is ten thousand dollars, for example, who will receive this amount? Will it be the issuing registry or the registrar? This is a question that needs to be answered. So if you have large savings, are being backed by investors or are willing to take out a mortgage, then you can play the domain game and possibly afford a new domain at a new gTLD. This is how the internet was taken.

When buying products or services, being the recipient of great customer service, is the key to success for establishing a brand. Especially in the arena of domain names, and website services, superior communication is the most valuable commodity. For any venture in the realm of technology, where complexities can seem overwhelming and jargon has its own specialized terminology, one should be sure to buy services and products from a company that cares and whose employees have great communication skills - above all others, the trait of patience.

Buying a domain name is a highly sophisticated process. Firstly, one must research key terms, and emerging trends, in the marketplace and then determine how a coined phrase can be generated, which would nicely fit into a domain name. Secondly, one needs to try to register the name and to obtain a suitable and relevant extension (DOT WHATEVER) for it. Buying the domain at the lowest possible price should be the prime directive, but one should be more focused on the registrar from whom one will purchase it. Support in forwarding the domain to your blog, or to a name server for hosting, can be a great exercise in learning for a novice to the world of internet technology. While for the seasoned web developer this would be a simple task. Either way, open communication with one's registrar is important. Real customer service includes good communicators, who will be of great value to one's sanity, in the seemingly complex process of buying and managing one's new domain.

One should do thorough research before utilizing the services of a so-called free website service and complimentary hosting. The terms of service need to be clearly defined at the onset to prevent any confusion later on. If you create a free website or receive free hosting, will you have access to the file manager where your website is hosted? Will you have permission to transfer your website to another host? What files will be exportable and which ones will be maintained with the hosted file? All of these questions should be asked before creating your website. Always read the terms of service and other related agreements from your service provider. There could be terms that would be of great value to use as the customer contained in the agreement for service. While these contracts are quite lengthy and perhaps intentionally so, one should spend the time to review them and know what one is actually to before just clicking the ok button.

Deciding whether one should pay an additional fee upon registration, for privacy on one's ownership of their domain, is only one of many concerns, which one will want advice on, from a customer service representative. Whether one should forward their domain with a temporary or permanent status and whether one should have subdomain forwarding are among many tasks to ponder. Another query is if forwarding should be done with masking or not. One will want to talk over all of these matters and many others with a technical expert. Usually, one can edit their contact details in the domain control panel, but it seems that some valid contact information must be listed there - as per the rules.

The rules do not seem, however, to dictate that one must forward their domain to a website, or blog that will be hosted, or to a free blogspot.

Here, in this decision, one can feel content in one's choice for redirecting their domain name. But one should be cautious as to how many domains one will direct to the same website, and be careful about syndicating the same post to many of one's own blogs. While one will want to get the word out, some search engines will penalize such efforts; by not listing the posting, or by ranking it very low in the search results. These are only some of the many questions, over which one might ponder, when entering the ***world of domains***. Most importantly, Customer Service is the Key to Success in the World of Domains.

FREE MARKET DOMAIN ILLUSIONS

It may perhaps be an illusion that there exists somewhere or anywhere a free market, in some democracy in the world. This is a bold statement and perhaps presumptuous.

But if there is a place in the world with a truly free market economy, then I would like to be the first to know about it. In many seeming free market economies there is much red tape that still restricts the buying, selling and trading of goods and services. As well there are monopolies that govern the marketplace and which form collective partnerships with related businesses to control the market.

One such example is the domain name industry. In this electronic realm of commerce there is almost no regulation. Registrars do as they please with domain names they sell. They can and do set the price of domain extensions in partnership with Registries. They limit the listing of domain names for auction on their websites. all the while allowing nearly identical domain names to be listed for sale on their portal.

This control and autonomous power of the Internet is due to the fact that the Internet is not regulated by the government. "The Obama administration is months away from deciding whether the United States Government will continue to provide oversight over core functions of the Internet and protect it from authoritarian regimes that view the Internet as a way to increase their influence and suppress freedom of speech," Cruz said in a statement."1

In the article on this link:
http://www.foxnews.com/politics/2016/06/09/obama-administration-backs-plan-to-relinquish-internet-control.html various details are provided, which explain how the US government will relinquish what remaining control it has over the Internet. Initially the plan was to cede control to ICANN,

which is a so-called not for profit agency with assets of $99.82 million USD and revenue of $72.02 Million USD as at 2011 (https://www.google.ca/?gws_rd=ssl#q=icann).

Now there are plans to let the United Nations govern the Internet. It is uncertain what this will mean for the World Intellectual Property Organization WIPO and its role in regulating internationally protected trademarks.

Now that we can be sure that there will be an increasing number of countries involved in Internet regulation, it is certain that no one will really know the rules of the game. Moreover, how can non profit organisations have assets of nearly $100 Million USD and revenues of more than $70 Million USD. It seems clear that no one is really overseeing the Internet, which is perhaps the largest business in the world that continues to grow at an ever-increasing rate daily.

Some domain Registrars boast of revenue of more than $1.05 Billion and some Registries, which own hundreds of the nearly 2000 new gTLDs (generic Top-Level Domains) have assets in the high Billions USD with expenditure cash of more than $100 Million USD.

Can we be sure, with all of the above said, that interests are being protected; as consumers or domainers (people who buy, sell and trade domain names)? If the domain name industry is for the most part unregulated or self regulated and the Internet will soon be totally regulated by an entity whose purpose is to govern international matters of peace and harmony, then who is 'minding the online store'?

1. http://www.foxnews.com/politics/2016/06/09/obama-administration-backs-plan-to-relinquish-internet-control.html

SEO CLASSIFIED FILES

Search Engine Optimization is a seemingly obscure phenomenon. Is it really as complicated as it seems? Perhaps SEO is a science. Every science has a system and sets rules or procedures used during the experimental process. Effective SEO requires logic principles and the proper application of defined processes. The first step is to register a domain name with Google Analytics and insert a Google Analytics' tracking code on your website. This is similar, in principle, to registering the address of a house in a new subdivision, with the relevant municipality where it is situated. The next step is to confirm the website address or domain name URL: Uniform Resource Locator with Google Webmaster Tools; either via a property ownership identifier via the registrar of the Generic Top Level Domain. You can also post a Google Webmaster Tools Meta Tag in the <head> section of the html or other code or script used to design your website.

After you have completed the confirmation steps successfully, as noted above, you will want to link the domain name or property between your Google Analytics and Google Webmaster Tools accounts. Creating and submitting a Sitemap for your website, is the next required step for maximum SEO results and top ranking on Google, as well as other Search Engines.

Once you have submitted the Sitemap, be sure to test it to ensure that there are no page display errors encountered by the Google robot that crawls your website. Next you will want to add a Robots.txt file to grant and / or limit access to various pages of your website. You may not want all pages crawled. If you have certain proprietary pages that contain confidential files or personal details, then you may restrict access to these pages. Also, if you have certain product pages that you only want to be made visible upon purchase of the electronic file, then you can input a Do Not Follow protocol in your Robots.txt file. You should test your Robots.txt file to be sure that it is functioning properly, with 'allow' or 'disallow' permission options, which will notify the robot whether or not it should have access to some or all pages of your website. You should then submit your website to be Crawled, using the 'fetch' and 'render' option. After your website has been fully rendered, you will want to submit it to be indexed in the Google Search Engine.

HOW TO BE NUMBER #1 ON GOOGLE

How to be number one on the Google search engine? How does one get listed at the top of all of the advertisements when a search is conducted for a product or service that one offers? Recently I spoke with a fine gentleman who has a top spot on Google. He has no formal technological training. But what he does have is persistence.

He constantly writes articles about a variety of topics and posts them on various websites throughout the internet or on the World Wide Web. Perhaps the latter more specifically explains the nature of search-ability and how our use of interconnected communication actually operates.

In all that I recall that he said he has written upwards of more than one thousand articles thus far. This fine gentleman explained to me that he will often submit articles to existing blogs, newspapers and other publications, online and in-print, asking only that they credit his blog with the authorship of the article. As a result, many internet surfers who read these articles are in-turn inspired to visit his blog. His blog is number one on Google.

He also has the top stop on YouTube. His videos are useful in helping novice blogspot developers to build and enrich their blog to maximize readership. It is perhaps due to this fine gentleman's knowledge of sales & marketing that he is able to hone his skills online.

Moreover, when I asked him for advice on how to increase visitors to my website and blog, he told me not to think in technical terms. Instead, he suggested that I consider what people want to read about. Trends in the media and in discussions on the internet on various blogs are the key topics of interest to readers. He also suggested that I create a video of my website / blog using a variety of software options and then post the video on

YouTube. I thought that he must be joking. In my own estimation, I did not believe that anyone would want to view a video of a website / blog on YouTube. But in my efforts to create a video of my website / blog and post it there, I came to realize that I was not the only person to utilize this marketing effort. Actually, this process of website / blog promotion is quite common.

There are some great websites which I discovered in my efforts to increase traffic to my website. I will share them with you now. One was suggested by the kind sir who has the #1 spot on Google. This website is Fiverr.com, is a virtual database of thousands of specialists in the fields of media and marketing who will help you to promote just about everything. The other website I came to discover is Wix.com, which is a free website building tool that also hosts your website. It comes complete with a variety of templates, according to your desired design style.

One other process that this top ranking search-engine-guru told me he employs to be among the top listed sites on the internet is that he creates advertisements for business and then contacts them to find out if his ads have resulted in inquiries. If so, then he pitches the companies in the following way. He tells them that he initially created the ad for them (free / complimentary), but if they would like to continue to benefit from the customer contacts resulting from this online promotional strategy, then they will need to pay for the ad. Based on the high volume of business generated from the ads, these companies are very grateful and willing to compensate the fine gentleman for his beautifully constructed ad. What an idea. No wonder why this man's blog has the highest number of views on the largest search engine in the world.

I hope that this advice helps you to grow and enhance your website / blog. While I do not have the #1 position on Google, I would certainly like to increase the number of visitors to my website.

TIPS TO INCREASE WEBSITE SPEED

This article is mainly for WordPress websites. If you want to be sure your website is fast enough, then you can utilize this free tool from Google: Page Speed Insights.

If after testing your website's speed, you may have decided that it does not load fast enough, then you can use this handy tool from Google to upload a Module to optimize your site automatically. Page Speed Modules.

We get you through the Internet labyrinth.Next you will want to figure out which plugins are slowing down your website. This plugin is a great tool for determining which plugins are costing you more resources than they are worth in terms of usefulness.
You can also test the cache on your website with this WordPress plugin: WP Super Cache
Before adding any plugins to your website you should verify that they have no malware or other issues, by testing them for WordPress Plugin Vulnerabilities, in the WPScan Vulnerability Database.

Backing Up your SQL Database is a must before adding any new content to your website, including plugins. You will want to ensure you are maximizing space in the server of your hosting account. Compressing images is a great way to save space. This plugin seems to work well: WPSmushIt. Files and content can also take up a lot of space in your hosting account. A great plugin to compress files is WPGzipNinjaSpeedCompression.

You may not realize that you have saved drafts and duplicate posts. A great way to clean up your database without running manual queries is by using this plugin: WP Optimize. Finally, you delete unnecessary plugins, content and files from, both your website and hosting account. In your hosting account you could have duplicate Databases and other files, which may be slowing down your website.

Any content, file or even unnecessary code can be causing your website to load more slowly than it should. If all else fails, contact an expert Webmaster for assistance. Web Design is part of ranking a website highly on the Internet organically. User experience is important to ensure that visitors stay on various pages of a website for a substantial period of time. This will keep the bounce rate to a minimum and build up a strong reputation for your website with Google and other Search Engines.

A fast loading website will increase the likelihood of visitors perusing various pages of your website.

DOMAIN INTERNET CHANGES

Domain names are all the hype today. Whether you are talking .club, condos, or .guru, among the currently available extensions on the market. But what about all of the domains that are coming soon? Close to 2000 possible extensions may one day be available for use.

If you buy a new domain name extension or gTLD (generic top-level domain) can you use it and / or sell it as you would with other extensions? It seems that the registries that are conjuring up these new novelty extensions are controlling the process of the entire life cycle for their gTLDs. They determine when the registrars can sell them, including pre-registration and priority registration and even auctions for competing bidders for the same domain name who priority registered a domain with different registrars. Can you imagine that there are auctions for domain names that are not even available yet? Domain names that have not yet been used for a website and have not even been available as forwarding domains are highly valued and can be sold, before they are yet bought.

What is the deal with the domain Internet changes? Is this madness? Possibly this domain name insanity is incurable. Trying to secure the right domain name can be maddening. Many registrar's may offer promotional gimmicks that seem to promise you a desired domain name at one of the many new extensions. But what can they really offer you other than notification, by email, when the gTLD becomes available? That is, unless you are willing and able to pay for pre-registration or priority registration (much more costly) and this is dependent upon the sunrise or release date of the domain name.

Domain names are now being screened by an intake clearing house to ensure that trademarks are respected and upheld by the trademark holder / owner. It used to be that someone could register any business name, as domain name, even if one did not own the business name proper - having registered it with the required regulatory authority. Perhaps the new extensions TLDs were created to ensure that rightful trademark owners can fairly register the business name as their own domain name.

But will this process actually restrict unlawful registrations across the board for all gTLDs? Or is the clearing house only monitoring and enforcing for requested gTLDs to ensure that trademark holders will gain a suitable gTLD for their business name? If so, how will this process be any different from the initial launch of the .com extension where some domainers opted to capitalize on acquiring namesakes of well known brands and then offering the gTLD for sale at an outrageously high price at auction?

HOW TO BE A DOMAIN PROFESSIONAL

Domaining is an intense process of contemplating, buying & selling great domain names. In this seemingly simple, but actually highly complex realm, acquiring and marketing your domain is a sophisticated process. Want to know how to be a domain professional? Firstly, you need to decide if you are going to create a short domain of one to two letters and such. Then you must evaluate if you should create a more specific longer phrase domain name that actually means something and is perhaps the name of a company or process. Next you have to buy it at the right price, which is not always the lowest cost. Since after you purchase the domain it will be locked with a registrar for sixty days and during that time period you will need to rely on the service and customer support of the registrar.

Therefore, you will want to buy from a dependable seller who will assist you once you have bought the domain. Particulars such as functionality of an email address and domain forwarding are considerations that you will want to take into account before you pay for your online address.

Secondly, how marketable is your newly acquired domain name? Can you resell it for more than you paid to buy it? If so, by what markup? Who is your intended demographic for sale? What sale price is reasonable? When listing your domain for sale it is a good idea to have a comprehensive concept to match the domain. Otherwise, unless the domain is ultimately catchy as a key phrase, no one will want to buy it for more than you spent to purchase it. Once aware of the domain name, a prospective buyer might opt to buy the same domain name with a varied extension, such as dot.org, dot.biz or others. Therefore, you should buy all of the possible extensions for your domain at the initial time of purchase or definitely before marketing your domain.

Thirdly, it is important to know if your domain name has value. There are websites that evaluate the worth of a domain. But it is more important to know the inherent value of the domain name to your intended buyers. Now that close to seven hundred new extensions will be released worldwide, having a great domain has never been easier. Many domain registrars are pre-registering customers for their dream domain name. At last count, one such registry had nearly two million pre-registrations. You should consider the best extension for your domain by utilizing part of your domain name as the extension itself.

Lastly, in this rigmarole of domaining, having the right budget is the key to being successful. After you have pre-registered for countless names, you will have to pay for them once they become available. Also, after you have purchased many domains, you need to be sure you will have enough money to buy more domains and to meet your general expenses. Having a reserve account for expenditures, in addition to investors and partners is a good idea. Even though you will need to share the potential profits, you will have more cushions on which to rely. It is important to note that the governing organization for domains has recently created a trademark clearinghouse. Therefore, it is wise to research the current usage of a phrase before buying it to avoid infringing on the intellectual property of someone else.

DOMAIN NAME MADNESS

Are you ready for the Domain Name Madness? With many new gTLDs being released over the next few weeks, many questions arise. One needs to know how one can acquire a new domain name, at one of the new extensions. Will the new extensions be affordable? Does one need to research potential trademarks, prior to applying for a new gTLD? These are some of the many questions that one should ponder, before paying for a pre-registration or priority pre-registration for a new gTLD.

Some registries will be pricing new gTLDs at $10,000 or more, for the first day of release; with the price dropping, by about a hundred dollars or so, each day thereafter. One golden rainbow of hope, in all of this domain name madness, is that registrar's will only be accepting, either one pre-registration or priority pre-registration for each gTLD. If one pre-registers for a new gTLD, one can receive a full refund, if one is not the successful purchaser of it. However, if one priority pre-registers a new gTLD one will likely receive a refund, less the cost of an application fee.

In all of this domain name madness, one must question: Who keeps all of the cash? If the same new gTLD is pre- or priority-registered with multiple registrars, then the gTLD will be put to auction. If one chooses to opt out of the auction, then will one receive a refund? Or will one be eligible for a refund, only if one is not the successful buyer?

To avoid competing buyers vying for the same gTLD, registries could post applications, from all registrars, for a new gTLD. Also, registries could, in cooperation with the Internet clearinghouse, post notices of trademark enforcements by companies who own a set trademark. Why should one mistakenly pre- or priority pre-register a domain name - and possibly bid on one at an auction - only to find out at a later date, that the domain was protected by a trademark, all along? Perhaps registries or registrars could post links (on their websites) to trademark databases for easy search-ability of protected names. There really needs to be clear governance of the Internet, which for the most part is unregulated, *to ensure that domain name madness can be made sane*!

    Clear governance of the Internet would be possible if one association oversaw the Internet. There is [ICANN](), but there is also the [World Intellectual Property Office]() and also [marcaria.com]() where you can search international trademarks and register your new domain names. For excellent reference on how to understand domain name governance you can review the book on the following link:
[International-Domain-Name-Law]()

INTERNET EXPANSION FUNDING

How will Internet expansion funding be provided? With many pre-registration registrars offering to pre-register a domain for one of the new extensions and charging fees upwards of a hundred and twenty dollars, one might need to take out a loan to be able to afford the domain names one wants to acquire. Are there, actually, brokers or lenders who will issue loans or credit to domainers for the purchase of a domain name? One lender that will grant a loan with the domain name as collateral is: Lend.Me. The domain name is used as collateral, similarly to house or property put up for a mortgage? While there are so many great new extensions and so many uncertainties about the actual cost to buy a new domain name for a new extension.

While there are clearly set prices for pre-registrations, there seems to be much ambiguity about the actual cost of a new domain name with one of the new extensions. Also, after pre-registration for a new domain extension there is no guarantee that once one has pre-registered that one will actually be able to buy their intended domain. Reasons for this abound with explanations such as there could be a bidding competition for the new domain at the new extension. Where many pre-registrants have pre-registered with various registrars for the same domain name, the domain name will be put to auction and then sold to the highest bidder. This process hardly seems fair.

Speaking of all things being unequal in the new domain name frenzy, if a company holds a trademark on a phrase then they can dispute the registration of a domain by someone else and also claim the domain name as their own. Therefore, if one really wants to guarantee that they will be the successful recipient of a certain domain name at a certain extension, then one only needs to register a trademark for the phrase – that is if the phrase is not already registered. This does not seem fair either. Where must one register a trademark, considering that the internet is global? Hence the phrase World Wide Web, which precedes most domain names in the URL bar.

If one is located in one country, does one have an obligation to register a trademark in their country of residence or in multiple countries? The domain name will be viewed online globally and the trademark could be infringed if the phrase in the domain name is broadcast on the internet. Moreover, can one register a trademark at a lower cost in a foreign country, which is not their country of residence, and also register a business associated with this trademark in that country and then be privy to the rights of a trademark holder. These are some of the many questions and concerns that remain, to be explained, during this frenzy of the Internet's largest expansion ever.

NEW gTLDs Trademark Concerns

New gTLDs trademark concerns are some of the issues to be resolved for the most prominent expansion of the Internet since its inception. If one owns a domain name; be it a dot.com or other extension, one wants to ensure that one is protected from trademark infringements, and defended against accusations of infringing on a trademark. If one does register a trademark in their country of residence, one is not necessarily protected against trademark issues in other countries. Even though the internet is a global environment, one's registration of a domain name does not guarantee that one has the right to use a business name or a set phrase. To be sure that one is not setting oneself up for trouble, one should perform trademark search before registering a business name, and prior to buying and using a domain name online.

Before registering any domain name, at any extension, one should thoroughly research the business name upon which the domain name is based. As well, one should retain the services of a noteworthy Intellectual Property Attorney who specializes in Trademarks and Copyrights.

The issue of trademark infringement arises for the same trademarked name. Also, if the same logo, or company image, is being represented, then there may be an issue for exploration. Potential concerns include: other similar trademarked names, in other languages, which when translated would be the same as the English equivalent. The Canadian Trademark website for registration is: cipo.ic.gc.ca/eic/site/cipointernet-internetopic.nsf/eng/wr01369.html. One should speak at length with a representative from this office, in addition to consulting with a lawyer, before applying for a trademark, and definitely before registering for and paying for one.

A savvy business person should consider that if one plans to have a website that will potentially sell digital goods to international clientele, then one is essentially operating in every country where one sells one's products. Therefore, one should research registered trademarks in all of the countries where one plans to sell one's goods. To create multiple-country trademark registrations one can utilize the services enabled by the establishment of the Madrid Protocol, which provides for international registration of a trademark.

For international trademark registration details – Madrid Protocol System - one should visit the main website for the World Intellectual Property Organization: wipo.int/madrid/en/. This website lists information about the registration of a trademark in 70, or so, international cities. This website lists workshops for intellectual property lawyers. It also displays listings of international expert attorneys who have extensive experience with international trademark matters.

Currently Canada is not a subscriber to Madrid Protocol Registration System. Over the next few years this may change. One can view a list of participating countries on the following link, by selecting to open the List of Members PDF: wipo.int/madrid/en/members/. Should one endeavour to register a trademark through this process one should definitely consult with and retain a recognized Intellectual Property Attorney. One who owns a domain name and who has a business that operates internationally may require international representation, in addition to a great global marketing campaign.

DOMAIN EXCHANGE

What is a domain name exactly? A set of words or a phrase, numbers or symbols or a mixture of all components, combined with an extension, known as Generic Top-Level Domain. There is even a day designated for Domain Names - known as World Domain Day: worlddomainday.com

Domain names are forms of online real estate, which are bought and sold, like commodities on a stock exchange: The Domain Exchange. Pre-Registration and Priority Registrations of new domain extensions are available at high prices to ensure the likelihood of one being able to obtain one's preferred domain name. If there are many bidders for a new Generic Top-Level domain, then the domain name will be auctioned. This entire procedure is in place even before the domain is even sold.

Once a domain name is sold, the successful purchaser can either utilize the domain name for a website or as a forwarding domain. Or one can list the domain name for sale at auction. An auction can last for a day or a week or for another set period. One can also list the domain for sale, as a Buy Now or Make Offer posting, with a minimum reserve price.

If one uses the domain name and then does not renew it, then one can lose the right to use it; but not immediately. Instead, one will receive emails from the registrar, indicating that one should renew the domain name by a certain date or lose it. Even at this point one can still sell the domain name or perhaps redeem it. If one waits too long to renew the domain name then the cost to use it can increase exponentially, and include an administration fee; as well as a renewal fee.

All of these bizarre processes would otherwise require an accredited course from a reputable school. Where can one take such a course, to become a domain name professional? Is there a College or University, which offers a course on *Domaining*? Should one need a license to buy and sell domains? They are a form of intellectual property. Some words or phrases could be trademarked and owned by a business. Perhaps a course would be a good idea.

Thorough research about various searchable trademark databases should be conducted before one begins purchasing domain names, especially if there is an advertising, copywriting or marketing focus to the domain names to be registered. This will ensure that one has done due diligence to avoid infringing on the intellectual property of another company, entity or person.

SOCIAL MEDIA SYNDROME

What exactly is social syndrome? There are so many social media outlets or platforms for expression of one's thoughts; such as: Twitter, LinkedIn, Facebook and Google Plus, among other super social media systems. These websites provide an opportunity for one to post updates on: one's daily activities, major milestones, sharing of one's achievements and advertising of products and services.

But are all these outlets user-friendly? Can anyone learn to utilize all of the benefits of these platforms? More importantly, if one is able to use these outlets, then is one doing so correctly? Is over posting common among members of these expression constructs?

While some people are able to write legibly and somewhat intelligently, they may not have the ability to convey their message appropriately. Concise language that is to the point and with the least amount of symbols is optimal for ensuring that one's intended meaning will be interpreted accurately. Posting at opportune times is essential to reach the maximum audience possible.

Perhaps for business promotion one should post between 5:00 and 5:30pm, at a time when the work day has concluded, but which is before dinner for more families. To share a celebratory message one should likely post it after dinner when people are satiated and craving social media. Is it a correct assumption that social media members will be most likely to use sites during transitional modes? Between meetings, after work, after dinner and just before going to bed are probably the most common periods for use of social media websites.

Do these electronic spaces of expression provide for increased communication? While some people may Tweet every hour and others may update their Facebook page constantly, are these people actually achieving maximum communication with other people? If you actually consider it you will realize that by spending so much time creating posts one is failing to actually connect directly with other people. Rather, one is more often interacting with a computer. Therefore, one could be less social by overusing social media.

Other than traditional posting on Twitter, users regularly submit content to be posted on Tumblr, StumbleUpon and LinkedIN. Internet users also share photos, sometimes too often on Instagram and Pinterest and overshare videos on Youtube and Vimeo. All of this excessive sharing online means less living in real time, by being active in the world. Meeting people and interacting with others is part of each person's duty to contribute to the global collective and the greater collective of one's own community.

WEBINERD

How many Webinars can there be in a week? Every day I receive invitations to attend webinars on a variety of topics. But how can I choose which one's are relevant to me personally? How can I determine which one's offer useful information, which could help me professionally? Perhaps some webinars may not offer useful information and instead are just platforms for sales pitches.

Should I prepare to take notes during the online seminar, or can I rely on the presenter to send me slides of his / her presentation? Will I receive a copy of the webinar I am unable to attend? To maximize one's time one should consider these points and perhaps e-mail the webinar organizer with specific questions before registering for a webinar. Webinars are an opportunity to interact with many participants via video conference. There is usually an initial presentation by a keynote speaker through video, or the presenter may speak, simultaneously during a slideshow. Usually webinars exist for the purpose of selling intellectual property, offering advice or selling an online lecture series. Webinars that have a fee may still offer an initial free seminar for the first meeting, as a sample. There is usually very little or no valuable information provided during the first complimentary session.

The sample session is a great opportunity for prospective students to quiz the host on the value of signing up, as well as a great time to inquire about the structure of the lecture series. Finding out if one will receive a copy of any slides or summaries of each daily or weekly lecture by e-mail is an important query. Also, it is important to know if one can view a recorded video of a missed lecture at a later time and date. Perhaps the host offers access to an account where there is a media library that contains all relevant presentation tools, to be accessible by paid members or students upon successful verified login.

During the initial complimentary session one will want to determine if the webinars will fit into one's schedule and ask if there are alternative schedules, if one is unable to attend at the initial set time. Even if there may be recorded sessions one will most likely want to be able to attend live seminars to be able to ask questions and to be able to hear in real time what other students are asking the host.

WORLD OF BLOGS

The other day I received a reply to an advertisement I had posted about my Writing Services for Blogs and Websites. Proposed payment per article was lower than I had anticipated. But this is not the first time I was offered less than I had believed to be the average rate for work in the Marketing Services Industry.

World of Blogs. The blogger explained that before any written work I submitted could be posted it would need to be screened on Copyscape.com. This website specializes in evaluating written materials to be posted online to verify that the copy is not plagiarized and does not infringe on anyone's intellectual property. When searching for this website I came across a similar Siteliner.com, which is also for reviewing written material and scrutinizing it for plagiarism. As well, the specialized tools on this site can scan your website and produce a report, which details the links on your website, informs you if they are functioning correctly or are broken and compiled in a list for your review.

When writing articles for blogs and websites you need to be aware of databases such as Knowem.com, which can help you to manage and secure your brand online. It also has a listing of all of the social media tools that you could ever want to promote your company on their networks page: Knowem.com/websites/all. If you are writing about a business and want to know where it has been featured on the internet there is a great website for you to utilize: Socialmention.com. It ranks online listings as positive, negative or neutral and lists how often the entity is mentioned, as well as how many authors have written about the topic of interest.

If you are aspiring to be a professional blogger or copywriter you need to consider what type of blog you will use to showcase your writing. Composing content on your blog or website is a great way to demonstrate your knowledge on a certain subject. Posting blogs often will grow your list of followers. Some blogs have IP addresses that make it easy to forward a domain name, while others only offer the option of a great blog title and easy to use functionality for design and widgets functionality. Definitely read online reviews about various blog hosts before creating your blog to determine if there are any restrictions for uploading images, and software add-ons to a page, or in a widget or as a link. Most importantly, research what SEO options the blog hosts provide for the listing and promotion of your blog in some or all search engines.

Also, when considering a title for your blog, first search domain registries to find out if a similar domain name is available. Likely a varied extension such as *.info* or *.org* might be available for your desired domain, even if the *.com* extension is taken. Before purchasing a domain name, thoroughly research the various domain registrars, to get the best price and the highest level of customer service. The lowest price is not always the best deal. Factors such as customer service, technical support and control panel tools for domain forwarding and management are more important than a low price. As well, the ability to transfer your domain and the cost for renewal are other important considerations. Lastly, inquire as to whether the registrar has an auction page to sell your domain and visit it prior to registering your domain.

WEBSITE SUCCESS TIPS

Do you have a blog or a website? Do you currently have a large following of subscribers? What if you quickly experienced a change in visitors or in ranking of your online portal? These help website success tips will help you to maximize your website's presence on the Internet.

Updates to Search Engine Optimization Tools, creation of new sitemaps and re-indexing by a Search Engine can affect the position of your online domain space. To be sure that you will be able to maintain your top spot and to continue to have regular daily visitors to your blog or website you need to diversify your marketing approach.

In addition to updating keywords, descriptions and Meta Tags as needed, you will also need to submit your website to Search Engines on a set schedule. Every month or so is a good strategy. Also you will need to compose great and intriguing content that gets people talking and sharing your posts on major social media outlets.

Be sure to have a Google Analytics account and to have your website properly tracked. Also, be sure your Google Webmaster account is appropriately linked to the account and connected to the relevant domain name. Requesting that your website be crawled is a good option. Hiring a competent Webmaster is probably the best idea.

You will need to do routine maintenance to stay in visible position on Google and other Search Engines. This work is time intensive so unless you have a lot of free time you should benefit from the expertise of a qualified Webmaster or SEO company.

AD WORDS OPTIONS

To be sure, you want to be found online for the right keywords, as you believe them to be in actuality. Whether you have chosen the correct keywords and / or description is another matter. Yes, these parameters influence your position on the Internet. But if you go the route of AdWords, then you might not care about these items.

There are factors you may want to consider before paying for ranking using AdWords. Firstly, if you have many impressions, but few clicks, then your organic ranking will be lowered. Organic ranking is where your website is really ranked by the Search Engine based on content, amount or number of words, keywords, descriptions, cross links, referral links and whether or not your website is responsive or mobile friendly.

If you utilize AdWords and do have many clicks for your ads, which results in visitors visiting your website, but leaving after a few seconds, then your bounce rate will be high. Having a high bounce rate will also lower your organic or real ranking. If you do not know the correct keywords for your industry, then you may purchase keywords from AdWords that are not relevant. This could result in visitors - who are not really looking for a company that provides the products or services offered by your company - finding your website and visiting it. While you may have increased your visitor rate, your bounce rate will be high and it is unlikely that you will convert any would-be potential customers, known as leads or referrals into actual sales.

To be successful with an AdWords campaign you need to have a reasonable budget to be able to afford the Pay Per Click Rate for the keywords you want to buy and use. The Pay Per Click rate will vary based on other companies bidding on the same keywords on the same day and or time of day. If you do not have a reasonable budget, then you will not be able to compete to secure the words you want at the price you can afford. Also, you will not be able to maintain a campaign, which would potentially yield results of visitors to your website.

If you are not knowledgeable about Search Engine Optimization, then you may want some help. If you would like some assistance with organically improving the ranking of your website, then please visit this link and review options BrandsWon.com

www.ingramcontent.com/pod-product-compliance
Lightning Source LLC
Chambersburg PA
CBHW071434220526
45469CB00004B/1532